Reycraft Books
55 Fifth Avenue
New York, NY 10003
Reycraftbooks.com

DEDICATED TO MY FAMILY. LET'S LEAP TOGETHER. —A.W.

Library of Congress Control Number: 2021923810

ISBN: 978-1-4788-7587-1

Photograph credits: Jacket Front: Francesco Tomasinelli/Science Source; Jacket Back Flap, Page 32B: Photo by Derek Whipple; Poster B: GFC Collection/Alamy; Poster C, E, Page 5B, E, H, CC, KK, UU, 16C, 21B, D, 29H, K, 31: Nature Picture Library/Alamy; Poster D: RooM the Agency/Alamy; Page 5F: Mark-Oliver Rödel; Page 5I: B. Trapp/agefotostock; Page 5N: Buiten-Beeld/Alamy; Page 5O: Morley Read/Alamy; Page 5V: Peter Steyn/ardea.com/agefotostock; Page 5Y, BB, YY: Dante Fenolio/Science Source; Page 5DD: Daniel M. Portik; Page 5GG: D. Bruce Means, Ph.D.; Page 7D: Candler Hobbs/Georgia Institute of Technology; Page 11B: James Christensen/Minden Pictures; Page 11D: Michael and Patricia Fogden/Minden Pictures; Page 12B: Dan Suzio/Science Source; Page 15: Danita Delimont/Alamy; Page 16B: Bazzano Photography/Alamy; Page 16D, 17: Greg Dimijian/Science Source; Page 19B: J.M. Storey, Carleton University; Page 19C: Nick Michaluk/Alamy; Page 19D: Panther Media GmbH/Alamy; Page 20A: Milan Zygmunt/Alamy; Page 20B: Imagebroker/Alamy; Page 21A: Courtesy Gérard Vigo; Page 21E: Daniel Borzynski/Alamy; Page 23A: Media Drum World/Alamy; Page 28C: Bill Gorum/Alamy; Page 29F: Dr. Paul A. Zahl/Science Source; Page 29I: Xinhua/Alamy; Page 32B: Photo by Derek Whipple; All other images from Shutterstock and Getty Images.

Illustration credits: Page 3, 5, 7, 9, 11, 13, 19, 21, 23, 25: JuanbJuan Oliver

Printed in Dongguan, China. 8557/0223/19911

10 9 8 7 6 5

First Edition Hardcover published by Reycraft Books 2022.

Reycraft Books and Newmark Learning, LLC. support diversity and the First Amendment, and celebrate the right to read.

RIBBIT!

The Truth About Frogs

ANNETTE WHIPPLE

WHO'S
HOPPING?

Poison dart frog
Dendrobatidae

THE LEAPING LEGS.

THE BULGING EYES.

THE STICKY TONGUE.

Frogs—they jump, climb, and swim.
They munch on insects and splash in ponds.
But these amphibians do so much more.

Leaping Legs

Scientists have found more than 7,000 kinds of us—and they find more than 100 new species every year. Maybe you'll find the next new frog.

Hop to it!

Red-eyed tree frog
Phyllomedusidae

What's The Difference Between
Frogs and Toads?

Forest toad
Bufonidae

Toads are frogs! Frogs often have smooth skin and lean bodies. They leap with long legs. Toads usually take short hops and have plump bodies with thick, warty skin.

But toads are still frogs. There is no scientific difference. Scientists put similar animals into groups called orders. Glass frogs, treefrogs, true toads, and 51 other groups make up the Anura order.

AMPHIBIANS

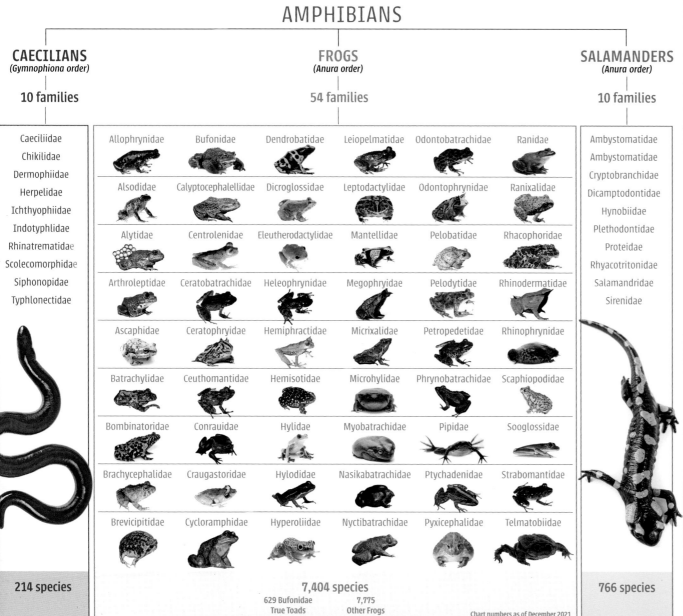

CAECILIANS *(Gymnophiona order)*	FROGS *(Anura order)*	SALAMANDERS *(Anura order)*
10 families	54 families	10 families

CAECILIANS
Caeciliidae
Chikilidae
Dermophiidae
Herpelidae
Ichthyophiidae
Indotyphlidae
Rhinatrematidae
Scolecomorphidae
Siphonopidae
Typhlonectidae

FROGS

Allophrynidae	Bufonidae	Dendrobatidae	Leiopelmatidae	Odontobatrachidae	Ranidae
Alsodidae	Calyptocephalellidae	Dicroglossidae	Leptodactylidae	Odontophrynidae	Ranixalidae
Alytidae	Centrolenidae	Eleutherodactylidae	Mantellidae	Pelobatidae	Rhacophoridae
Arthroleptidae	Ceratobatrachidae	Heleophrynidae	Megophryidae	Pelodytidae	Rhinodermatidae
Ascaphidae	Ceratophryidae	Hemiphractidae	Micrixalidae	Petropedetidae	Rhinophrynidae
Batrachylidae	Ceuthomantidae	Hemisotidae	Microhylidae	Phrynobatrachidae	Scaphiopodidae
Bombinatoridae	Conrauidae	Hylidae	Myobatrachidae	Pipidae	Sooglossidae
Brachycephalidae	Craugastoridae	Hylodidae	Nasikabatrachidae	Ptychadenidae	Strabomantidae
Brevicipitidae	Cycloramphidae	Hyperoliidae	Nyctibatrachidae	Pyxicephalidae	Telmatobiidae

SALAMANDERS
Ambystomatidae
Ambystomatidae
Cryptobranchidae
Dicamptodontidae
Hynobiidae
Plethodontidae
Proteidae
Rhyacotritonidae
Salamandridae
Sirenidae

214 species

7,404 species
629 Bufonidae
True Toads

7,775
Other Frogs

Chart numbers as of December 2021

766 species

Big-eyed tree frog
Arthroleptidae

How Do FROGS EAT?

Frogs usually feast on insects, but they'll eat whatever critters fit in their mouths. Most frogs snatch dinner with their tongues. Some grab prey with their front legs.

Northern leopard frog
Ranidae

The northern leopard frog spots its prey. The frog flips out its tongue. The spit on it acts like glue, and the insect can't get away. The frog pulls dinner inside its mouth. The frog closes its eyes. Blinking helps it swallow. Its eyes push the food down to the stomach.

Argentine horned frog
Ceratophryidae

The South American horned frog sits and waits. The horned frog spots and tackles a small mouse. Into the mouth the prey goes— whole and alive.

Leaping Legs

My Bufonidae toad family captures meals faster than other frogs. *That makes us TOAD-ally awesome!*

7

What Sounds Do Frogs Make?

Frogs fill warm nights with sounds. Male frogs have a lot to say because they're trying to get the attention of a mate. Each frog species has its own call.

Indian bull frog
Latrodectus

Squirrel tree frog
Hylidae

American toad
Bufonidae

Northern spring peeper
Hylidae

Wood frog
Ranidae

American toads trill.

Spring peepers chirp.

Wood frogs quack.

Did you think all frogs ribbit?
Nope!
Movies and books fooled you and made Pacific chorus frogs like me famous. We're the only ones that
RIBBIT.

To make a call, a male's neck expands like a balloon. The vocal sac (or sacs) inflates to work like an amplifier. The frog keeps its mouth and nostrils closed as it calls. It's exhausting but worth the work to get a mate.

9

What Are Frog Eggs Like?

Rana temporaria
Ranidae

10

Many frogs lay eggs in large masses. Toads lay chains of eggs that look like floating necklaces. Most frogs lay their eggs in water. But some frogs lay eggs in special ways.

The túngara frog builds a foam nest for its eggs. The outside of the nest hardens in the water, but the inside stays moist.

The climbing mantella of Madagascar lays a single egg in a tree hole filled with water. After the tadpole hatches, the mother feeds it some of her extra eggs.

The female dwarf marsupial frog carries 6–10 eggs on her back. When the tadpoles hatch, she takes them to water.

Some frogs lay just a few eggs, but the cane toad lays about 30,000 eggs at a time.

Leaping Legs

My red-eyed tree mama laid our eggs under this leaf.
Now that we have hatched, it's time for our big splash!

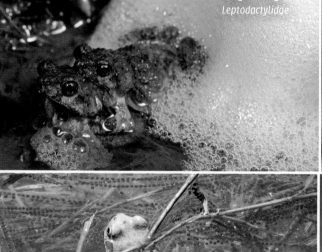

Túngara frog
Leptodactylidae

Climbing mantella of Madagascar frog
Mantellidae

Cane toad
Leptodactylidae

Dwarf marsupial frog
Hemiphractidae

11

American bullfrog
Ranidae

How Do
TADPOLES GROW?

Typically, tadpoles hatch from frog eggs after 1–3 weeks. They have gills to breathe in water. Their long tails make them look like fish, but they're not fish. They're frog larvae. The larvae must change to become frogs.

Most tadpoles eat lots of plants and algae. All the feasting helps them to grow quickly and change.

Tadpoles often become froglets in just a few weeks. Eastern spadefoots change in as little as two weeks, but the six-inch American bullfrog tadpoles can take three years to become a froglet.

Legs grow.

Lungs develop.

Tails disappear.

They lose their gills.

The changes from egg to frog is a process called metamorphosis.

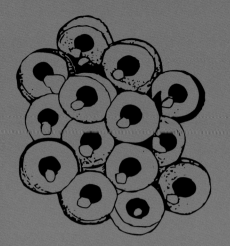

METAMORPHOSIS
FROM EGG TO FROG

Most frogs change from egg to tadpole to froglet to frog in a process called metamorphosis. The time it takes to complete metamorphosis can be days or years. It depends on the species.

Fertilized Egg

DAY 1

Egg

DAY 3-4

Egg with tail bud

Tadpole Early Stages

DAY 6

Tadpole with external gills

DAY 9

Tadpole with internal gills

DAY 12

Tadpole with operculum

Tadpole Late Stages

DAY 70

Tadpole with hind limbs

DAY 84

Tadpole with forelimbs

Froglet

DAY 84+ Tadpole metamorphosis

Adult Frog

Rana temporaria (actual size)
Ranidae

2-4 YEARS

Leaping Legs

I hatched and then wriggled onto my mama's back. Since poison-dart frogs lay eggs on land, she hopped me to water.

It's froggy-back time!

13

WHERE DO FROGS LIVE?

Strawberry poison frog
Dendrobatidae

Zaire dwarf clawed frog
Pipidae

Wood frog
Ranidae

Pickerel frog
Ranidae

Most frogs live in wet areas like swamps, marshes, and seasonal ponds. Others dwell in fields, forests, and even deserts.

American bullfrogs and Zaire dwarf clawed frogs rarely leave the water, even as adults.

Wood frogs prefer marshes and woodlands, but they live as far north as the treeless Arctic Circle.

Pickerel frogs spend their summers in grassy fields, forests, and even caves. They migrate to water to breed.

American bullfrog
Ranidae

Leaping Legs

Swimmers, learn from the best!
We used the frog kick first. In fact, we invented it!

How Do Some Frogs Live Underground?

Desert dwellers burrow underground to stay cool.

Namaqua rain frogs live in the South African desert. They leave their sandy burrow to eat or call to a mate during fog or rain. Females lay eggs in underground nests.

Couch's spadefoot toads burrow several feet deep for 9 months of the year. They surface to breed and eat after heavy rains. A big meal of termites can be enough food for an entire year.

Great basin spadefoot toad
Scaphiopodidae

Namaqua rain frog
Brevicipitidae

Great basin spadefoot toad
Scaphiopodidae

Leaping Legs

Dig this!

We spadefoots survive drought with a mucous cocoon. All snug and slimy, we go into a deep rest called estivation. It's like hibernation but in the summer.

WHY DON'T FROGS FREEZE TO DEATH?

American toad
Bufonidae

Leopard frog
Ranidae

Wood frog
Ranidae

Leopard frogs survive the winter by hibernating in the water of a pond or lake. Their skin absorbs oxygen from the water.

American toads dig backward to burrow deep within the ground. They hibernate below the frost line where the soil doesn't freeze.

Some frogs, such as wood frogs and spring peepers, freeze in the winter—and survive. The sugar in their blood acts like antifreeze. It keeps the frogs alive until they thaw in the spring.

American toad
Bufonidae

Frozen frog in its winter habitat.

Leaping Legs

Leaf litter keeps us cozy during cold months. Leave some leaves behind for us. If you clean them all up, we might

CROAK!

19

How Do Frogs PROTECT THEMSELVES?

Many frogs are hard to spot. Their skin color camouflages them. But if danger comes, frogs often leap away from predators. Other frogs react in unique ways.

A rain frog squeaks and inflates its body to tell predators to back off.

The pebble toad curls into a ball and rolls away when a tarantula approaches it.

Wallace's flying frog escapes by gliding from tree to tree.

The eyes of a red-eyed tree frog close while it sleeps during the day. When it senses danger—

Vietnamese mossy frog
Rhacophoridae

20

Pebble toad
Bufonidae

Wallace flying frog
Rhacophoridae

Leaping Legs

I'm bold.
I'm bright.
I'm beautiful!
Predators see my colors and
know I'm poisonous.

I'm un-FROG-getable!

POP!

Its red eyes startle the
predator. Then it has the
chance to get away.

Red eyed tree frog
Phyllomedusidae

Are Frogs Important To People?

Australian green tree frog
Pelodryadidae

Dumpy tree frog
Hylidae

Texas toad
Bufonidae

Leaping Legs

Want to keep us hoppy?
Always return us to the same exact place where you found us.

Frogs are an important part of our natural world. During their life cycle, frogs play the role of both predator and prey. One frog can eat more than a thousand insects in a year, but an American toad can eat 1,000 insects in a single day. Frogs don't just eat; they're also eaten. They are essential meals for snakes, lizards, and birds.

Frogs are important to the world of science, too. Doctors use frogs to study cancer and pain treatment. Researchers use frogs to understand chemical testing.

As people clear land for homes, roads, and businesses, frogs lose their habitats. Their breeding grounds are in trouble. That means less frogs. Today about one-third of all amphibians (mostly frogs) are at risk of becoming endangered or extinct.

When people keep frogs and their habitats safe, more frogs grow with...

THE LEAPING LEGS.

THE BULGING EYES.

THE STICKY TONGUE.

AND THAT'S THE TRUTH ABOUT FROGS.

23

How Can I See Frogs?

Before you look for frogs, learn which frogs are local to your area. You'll often hear frogs before you see them, so listen to recordings of their calls. Then you can recognize the frogs by their sounds. Your local nature center or herpetological society might help.

- **Look in the evening or at night.** Head outside to a marshy area or pond during mating season (often spring or early summer). You'll hear more frogs after dark since most frogs are nocturnal. If you want to see even more frogs, go on a rainy night. Remember your flashlight.

- **Be quiet.** Frogs stop calling when they sense a predator.

- **Sit still.** Plan to sit or stand still at the side of the pond while you watch for movement. When a frog no longer senses danger, it'll call again and be easier to spot.

- **Take binoculars.** Even if the frogs are only 10 feet away, you'll be able to see the details of their bodies if you use binoculars in daylight.

- **Ask around.** Let others know you want to see frogs. Ask others if they know of any spots where you can see or hear frogs.

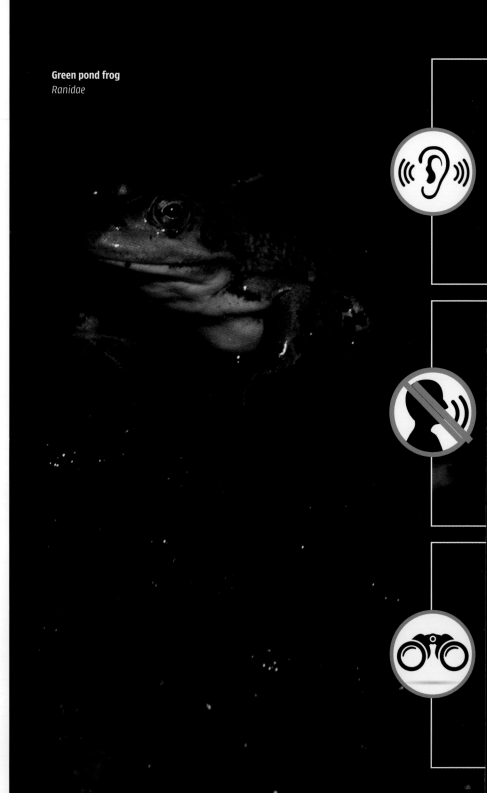

Green pond frog
Ranidae

Can I Have A Pet Frog?

Keep frogs safe.
If you want a pet frog, be sure it was bred in captivity. Don't take a frog (or an egg or tadpole) from the wild without talking to an expert.

Research more about frogs.
Frog owners need to know a lot about frogs before considering having a pet frog. Read many books. Ask other frog owners about their experiences.

Commit to your frog.
Some frogs live for more than 20 years in captivity. They cannot be released in the wild when no longer wanted as a pet, so you must be prepared for a long-term commitment.

Be responsible for your frog.
Caring for a frog is a lot of work. If you're uncertain if you're ready to own a frog, consider pet sitting others' amphibians to enjoy the animals without the commitment.

FROG

FACT OR FICTION?

Know the truth! Which of these froggy rumors are true, and which are false?

Let's find out!

Holding frogs doesn't hurt them.

Sometimes true and sometimes false!

Squeezing a frog can hurt it. Gently hold a frog around its middle—not by its legs. Amphibians breathe through their skin, so wash your hands before holding one. You'll also want to wash up afterward to prevent spreading viruses between animals.

European green toad
Bufonidae

Toads give you warts.

False!

Toads may be bumpy, but they don't give warts to humans. The bumps on our skin are caused by the virus human papillomavirus.

American toad
Bufonidae

Frogs pee on you.

True!

Frogs, and especially toads, pee as a defense mechanism. While this is not harmful, it often surprises predators just like it's supposed to do.

Red-eyed tree frog
Phyllomedusidae

Bullfrog tadpole

A tadpole you find in the wild makes a great pet.

False!

Unless you talk to a wildlife expert, do not keep a wild frog (at any stage) as a pet.

Frogs always live in water.

False!

All frogs need water, but they live in a variety of places. Aquatic frogs spend their lives in water. Terrestrial frogs dwell on the ground. Arboreal frogs live in trees.

Australian tree frog
Pelodryadidae

Tomato frog
Microhylidae

Herpetologists study frogs.

Emerald Glassfrog
Centrolenidae

True!

The scientists who study reptiles and amphibians are called herpetologists. They find more than 100 new frog species each year.

Frogs are poisonous.

Sometimes true and sometimes false!

Some frogs are perfectly safe to eat—even for us. Many people fry and eat the legs of the American bullfrog. Other frogs are poisonous.

Brazilian yellow head frog
Dendrobatidae

Blue dyeing dart frog
Dendrobatidae

Freaky, Funky
FROGS

With more than 7,000 kinds of frogs around the world, they have some amazing differences. Check out these unique frogs.

Great Plains frogs' long trills can last more than a minute.

Red striped poison dart frog
Dendrobatidae

African clawed frogs have no tongue and rarely venture on land.

Cane toads have the fastest tongues and capture prey in about 1/10 of a second.

Glass frogs have transparent skin, so you can see their organs.

Golden dart frogs are the most toxic of all frogs.

Goliath frogs can weigh over 7 pounds (3.3 kilograms) and measure more than a foot (32 centimeters).

Male **hairy frogs** don't have true hair, but they have hair-like structures on their back legs.

Male **midwife frogs** carry a string of eggs around their hind legs and keep them moist.

Actual size

Monte iberia dwarf frogs and *Paedophryne amauensis* are tied for the smallest frogs, both measuring less than 3/8 inch (1 centimeter) long.

Vietnamese mossy frogs live in wet caves and tree cavities and look like they're covered with moss.

Wallace's flying frogs leap, glide, and parachute up to 50 feet (15 meters) through the air.

DIY Toad House

The sun can dry out the skin of frogs if they don't have shade and water. Create a house to offer shade to your fantastic froggy friends.

Materials Needed:

- newspaper or other protective covering
- clay flower pot
- acrylic paint
- paintbrushes
- clear acrylic sealer

What to Do:

❶ Prepare a painting area by protecting all surfaces with newspaper. (Acrylic paint stains.)

❷ Use the brush and paints to decorate the outside of the clay flower pot. Allow the paint to dry completely.

❸ Apply a layer of clear acrylic sealer. Allow to dry completely.

❹ Choose your toad house's location. It should be a damp, shady spot. Places near water sources like a sprinkler, gutter downspout, and creek are options.

❺ Turn the pot on its side. Bury one side of the pot in soil. Place soil and leaf litter inside the pot so visitors can cool off during the heat of the day.

❻ Be patient as you wait for froggy friends to find the toad house.

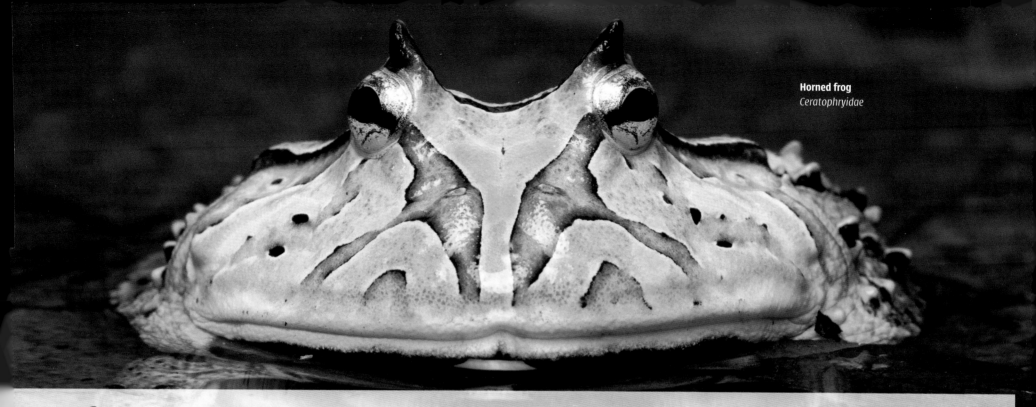

Horned frog
Ceratophryidae

GLOSSARY

algae: living things in the water that can be too small to see

amphibian: a cold-blooded animal that breathes through gills early in life and develops lungs later

antifreeze: a chemical that prevents liquid from freezing

burrow: (noun) an underground home made from a tunnel; (verb) to dig or live in an underground hole

camouflage: the natural coloring of an animal that makes it hard to be seen

drought: a long period of time without rain

estivation: the act of an animal sleeping deeply to survive summer

froglet: a small, young frog

gills: the organ that some animals use to breathe underwater

habitat: where a plant or animal usually lives

hibernation: the act of an animal sleeping deeply to survive winter

larvae: the young form of an insect or amphibian

metamorphosis: the process in which frogs, insects, and some other animals develop and change

migrate: to move from one area to another temporarily

predator: an animal hunting another animal for food

prey: the animal hunted by another animal for food

species: a specific group of similar animals

Some Helpful Websites

Herpetology is the study of reptiles and amphibians. Learn more about frogs from these websites.

www.amphibiaweb.org

www.eol.org

www.musicofnature.com/videos/

www.aza.org/frogwatch

www.ssarherps.org

https://animaldiversity.org

31

Meet Annette Whipple

Annette Whipple doesn't see many amphibians in her backyard, so each frog visitor delights her. She is the author of more than ten fact-filled children's books, including The Truth About series featuring owls, dogs, and spiders. Annette celebrates curiosity and inspires a sense of wonder while exciting readers about science and history. When Annette's not reading, writing, or doing author visits, you can find her hanging out with her family in Pennsylvania.